I0505307

DAY TRADING 2020

A Comprehensive Beginner's Guide to Day Trade for a Living, Save Time, Reduce Your Risk, Increase Your Earnings and Become Financially Free in 2020

Nobert Young

TABLE OF CONTENT

Introduction

Not everyone who ventures into day trading is successful; in fact, statistics show that 90% of people who venture into day trading fails. To break down this figure, 80% of day traders lose their money, 10% breakeven while the remaining 10% consistently makes a gain. It is important to note that this statistic has nothing to do with the trader's intelligence, gender, age, or geographical region.

Before you start to day trade, you need to know why these day traders fail so that you can avoid the mistakes they made. Day traders lose money because they fail to manage risks, invest in the right stocks, control their emotions, follow the rules of a working strategy, or find proper entries & exits. Everyone wishes to be among the 10% that are constantly making a gain, but not everyone wants to put in the effort and time needed to achieve this success.

In this book, you will learn trading techniques that have worked for me in achieving profits. I will also teach you the fundamental concepts of day trading. We will begin by exploring reasons most day traders fail as well as

4

what makes the remaining 10% constantly make profits. Then you will learn how to choose the right stocks, how to manage risks, how to control your emotions while trading, and how to enter and exit trades. This book will guide you and teach you all you need to know to maximize your profits while day trading.

Chapter 1: Basics of day trading

In time past, before personal computers, instant information, internet connectivity, and high-tech software, several brokerage firms employed veteran traders to interpret their stock transactions. These traders were called tape readers. The tape readers would indicate the price pattern and model of each trades on stock tickers with the hope of finding opportunities for fast profits. *A stock ticker is a price report of certain stocks, which is consistently updated all through the trading session.* If the newest trade of a certain stock is completely different from recent trades either in volume or price, tape readers would automatically assume that some insiders took secret actions before a piece of news that could affect the company's stock went public. Based on this, tape readers then take swift actions with the hope that their prediction works in their favor.

In recent times, in place of the stock ticker, we have an enormous electronic network that is robust enough to analyze and report trade data all over the world. This technology has replaced the pattern at which the investment industry works, bringing about a unique position in this dispensation's landscape, which gives us what we know today as day trading.

Day trading can be a very lucrative career once you do it the right way. However, it can be somewhat burdensome for beginners and novices, particularly for traders who do not have a well-mapped out strategy. Besides, even the most experienced day traders can shudder and experience losses from time to time. Let's now look at what day trading is all about.

What is Day trading?

Day trading is not in any way and has never been the same as investing. Investing, which is long term, consists of entering trades that remain open for months and even years while waiting for the trade to accumulate profit.

Day trading, on the other hand, involves buying and selling securities within a 24-hour interval (a single trading day). While day trading can happen in any marketplace, it is more common in stock markets and foreign exchange. Day traders use short-term trading strategies and high amounts of leverages to seize the opportunity of small price movements in extremely liquid currencies or stocks.

Day Trading is a predominant practice among traders who want to be active in the market and trade for gains. One significant benefit of day trading is that you don't have to carry any form of overnight risk. You are free to close out your position every day; that way, you won't have to worry about gaps in price when security closes up and then opens up the next day.

With day trading, you can trade almost any security, stock, or currency pair, so it's your choice to choose from numerous options available. The fundamental concept of day trading is that you take smaller trades and move in and out of the market as fast as you can since you don't occupy long trading positions, and your risk is lesser on every trade. The snag here is that you may get caught up in some small tight ranges of stock movement and attract a variety of small stop-outs.

Benefits of Day Trading

Placing trades throughout the day, actively observing every movement of the market, and making fast money are all appealing aspects of day trading. Below are some benefits of day trading:

Flexibility

Day trading gives you enough time to research, and it also offers a flexible work schedule. You can plan out how you desire each week to go. You also have the freedom to choose how much money you want to spend on a transaction per time.

Euphoria

The excitement and thrill of making big profits on your own cannot be over-emphasized. This is why daily trading can be addictive: you will earn money, learn more, challenge yourself to do better, and ultimately get good at trading. Daily trading can be quite dangerous, but consistency and putting in the right efforts will help you to learn the nitty grittiest of the process.

Great learning opportunities

Daily trading gives you more opportunities to determine market conditions and learn how to make money in the market using various approaches. As you proceed, you will be able to pick your best strategy out of all the different available options. Besides, many key advisors provide investors with the best trading tips, including stock futures hacks and intraday tips, to increase the trader's profit.

Independence

As a day trader, you are your own boss. You do not need to leave your home to go to an office location or follow deadlines and instructions to make a living except for personal limits and rules that you set for yourself. Working from home also reduces transportation costs. This freedom gives you the chance and time to engage in other matters. Nevertheless, respect your business every day and invest the time and effort you need to succeed.

Equipment and Software for Day Trading

Before you can begin to day trade for a living, you need the tools listed below:

- **A reliable and speedy internet connection:** Day traders need to use a minimum of ADSL or a Cable type of internet connection. We have varying internet speeds depending on the type of service you are on, so you need to go for a minimum of a mid-range internet package.

Working on the web with multiple web pages open as well as applications running in the background that use internet connection may affect the speed of your system and, in turn, cause your trading platform not to update as quickly as it should. I will advise that you begin with mid-range internet package and adjust your internet speed as needed. You cannot day trade successfully with a sporadic internet connection.

- **A laptop or computer:** Although it is better to have two monitors, it is not a major requirement. Your computer needs to have sufficient memory and a fast processor to avoid any crashes or lagging when you begin to run your trading programs. While you do not have to go for the most expensive computer, you should not go for the cheapest either. Computers and software continue to change and update; you need to ensure that your computer keeps up with the times. Using a slow computer can be costly, especially if it crashes in between trades; the slowness can cause you to get stuck in trades or even miss important trades.

- **A trading platform that suits your trading style and market:** When you first begin to day trade, getting the perfect platform shouldn't be your primary goal. Because you are just starting or new in the trade, you may not have a well-developed trading style from the beginning. So, it is normal for you to change your trading platform occasionally, or you may see the need to change how the trading platform is designed to accommodate your trading progress. There are several platforms available for trading stocks. NinaTrader is one of the popular platforms for futures and forex traders. You can download any of the trading platforms and try them out. Your broker will also recommend some of these platforms to you, and you can pick your preference after trying out several platforms.

- **A broker:** Your broker charges a fee or commission to help you facilitate your trades. Usually, daytraders always want to go for brokers with low fees as high commission costs can drain the profits gotten from a day's trading. But this may not always be the best option. The most important thing is to get a broker that will be able to support you when needed, even if you have to pay a few cents extra, so long as the company can help you to save hundreds or even thousands of dollars when you experience computer meltdown and not able to get out of your trades. That said, major banks that offer trading accounts do this at a very high fee for the same service that you can get from smaller brokers with commission structures and more customizable fees for day traders.

Chapter 2: Why Do Most Traders Fail?

You may have heard that most people who venture into day trading fail; in fact, 90% of traders fail to make any profit. Before you can be successful in trading, you need to do what other day traders are not ready to do. You may be asking how an inexperienced person can achieve much with all the overload of information out there. In this section, we will discuss the reasons most traders do not consistently make profits and what you need to do not to fall into the 90% category. You will also learn the steps that the 10% successful traders take that makes them successful at day trading.

Now let us go into the major reasons why day traders fail.

1. Lack of knowledge about day trading

This is the biggest reason most traders fail to make money when trading. Another reason for failure is poor education as people go to the wrong places to look for education and so end up with poor or wrong information. Several people refer to themselves as traders just because they buy and sell shares. However, the majority of these people do not know anything about analyzing the stocks or trades that they buy and sell. Several of them have little or no idea how to interpret a chart. They rely on reports gotten from websites or newspapers and occasionally review online charts with their broker. They also have no trading plan designed, neither do they understand what money management is all about.

An educated trader, on the other hand, knows how important it is to have a profitable trading plan, they also analyze stocks before they buy and sell, and they are skilled at managing their trades. Most importantly, educated traders have strong money management rules like position sizing and stop-loss, which helps them to maximize profit and reduce their risks.

2. Unrealistic trading expectations

Day trading comes with its own level of risk. Yet, several traders want to take higher risks with the belief that they have all it takes to trade and make immediate profits after attending a weekend course or reading a few books. Most traders want instant gratification and plunge into the market head-first, using complex strategies and believing that their efforts will yield them instant profit. These traders tend to lose their savings because of these unrealistic expectations. While its important to have trading knowledge, you also need to know how to apply this knowledge.

During a bull market, several people benefit based on luck and not because of proper knowledge. A strong bull market can hide the lack of knowledge and mistakes in judgment, which is why no one should call himself or herself a successful trader until he has traded for more than two years.

Several people want to learn how to trade in an easy, quick, and cheap way. If that sounds like you, it means that you may be part of the 90%. In reality, you can not go to a doctor who got his certification just by attending a weekend workshop, neither will you allow your kids to get on a bus if the driver tells you he only learnt how to drive by reading a book.

To graduate from the university, the student goes through rigorous studies and examinations for three to four years. Similarly, day trading is a business that you should treat professionally. The majority of day traders fail because they do not see day trading as a business and so, do not accord it with the needed respect and seriousness.

Before one can be an educated trader, you need to combine experience with a high level of knowledge. If not, the chances that you will succeed in day trading will be very slim.

3. The psychology factors affecting your trading

Its one thing to learn how to trade and another thing to understand your psychology, which is the harder part of trading. While some traders fail for lack of knowledge, others fail because of their trading psychology.

The psychology or attitude of a trader determines how they approach their trading. The emotions of greed and fear drive both investors and traders alike, and without proper education, these emotions can cause the trader to make costly mistakes. Fear is one big enemy to those who want to trade, it is even stronger than greed, and it comes as a result of lack of confidence in the trader's trading plan, lack of knowledge, as well as a trader's inability to successfully execute his trading plans.

Newbies or beginners in day trading, out of fear, exit profitable trades too early to avoid losing their profit.

4. Over Trading

It is human nature to abuse opportunities. People often overtrade every single day, all in the name of squaring up the losses faced in previous trades. By overtrading, day traders invite more losses than earnings. Of course, there's a possibility of making more while there's also the possibility of losing more. The maximum you should alternate is 1-2 trades per day. The moment you start trading greater than 4-5 times, almost certainly, you're going to lose some streaks. Now I don't mean to say that it's impossible to keep winning and that you will fail at every trade, in fact, there's a possibility that you may profit from all the five trades. But the chances that you will loss when overtrading is higher than the chances of winning. If you don't overtrade, you increase your chances of winning on a margin of 80-90. Plus, overtrading infuse emotions in the trader, and once emotions set in, you begin to lose your sense of judgement and objectivity.

5. No trading plan

A trading plan ushers the deal in the right direction. This includes everything from entry, exit, risk management, trading markets, timeframe, and position size – see it as a success plan. It is almost impossible for two traders to trade with the same trading plan as they have different levels of risk, and their nature also differs. Most traders do business without having a trading plan, and the simple truth Is wIthout a tradirıg plan, you're simply trading without a goal and direction, which inevitably will lead to potential losses.

6. **Not enough researching**

Another reason day traders fail is they don't take time to do extensive research on the intricacies of trading and the strategies applicable. Going the extra mile, and engaging on extensive research is very paramount to get the best out of day trading. Whatever strategy you'll end up utilizing must be well researched, understood, and analyzed before you begin to use it.

Basic Rules to Succeed at Trading

There are three basic rules to become a successful trader. Let's summarize it to say that the equation for successful trading is :

Experience + Knowledge + Effort = Success

There is no full-time trader who constantly makes a profit that got there through luck. All successful traders followed the simple steps below:

1. They sought and acquired knowledge.
2. As soon as they got the required knowledge, they developed their experience.
3. After sorting the two steps above, they then put in efforts to achieve their trading goals.

One statistic states that before a trader can fully learn to trade, he or she must have been in the market for two to five years. There are no two ways about this; you cannot substitute hardwork, neither are there any shortcuts to becoming a competent and professional trader. Self-education, in reality, requires that you put in the work and the commitment. This does not mean that you have to be a rocket scientist or a genius to achieve constant profit when trading.

When To Day Trade

As a day trader, whether a pro or a beginner, you need to be consistent. The best way to achieve consistency is to trade at the same hours every day. While there are day traders who trade for a whole regular session (9:30 a.m. to 4 p.m. EST for the US stock market), the majority of traders trade for some hours in the day.

Below, I have listed the hours you should focus on:

- For day trading futures, the best time to trade should be around the opening. An excellent opportunity to day trade futures usually begins a bit earlier than that of the stock market. For futures, you should concentrate on trading between 8:30 a.m. and 11 a.m. EST. This market has its official closes at varying times, but the last hour of trading in a futures contract also offers sizeable moves that day traders can capitalize on.

- If trading stocks, the best time to day trade is within the first one to two hours after the opening, that is, 9:30 a.m. to 11:30 a.m. EST. This period is the most volatile time of the day and offers traders the biggest price moves and very high profit potential. The last trading hour of the day is also another good time to trade as some sizable moves occur within this period, i.e., 3 p.m. to 4 p.m. EST. However, if you want to trade for only one to two hours, let it be during the morning session.

- The forex market is open for trading 24 hours daily during the week. The most popular day trading pair is the EURUSD. Its most volatile time of the day is between 0600 and 1700 GMT, which is the best time for day trading. Another very popular and active time for day trading is 1200 to 1500 GMT, as there are usually big price moves during this period. Within this time, both the US and London markets are open, trading the US dollar and the Euro.

Successful day traders do not necessarily trade all day as they achieve more consistency by sticking to trading for two to three hours each day.

Chapter 3: How Day Trading Works

Day Trading vs Swing Trading

Before you begin to trade, you need to determine how active you want to be. You need to ask yourself questions like: how much time do I have at hand, and what are my current responsibilities? Your answers to these questions will help you to decide if you want to trade daily or if you want to buy and hold for some days or weeks.

There are two groups of active traders: the day traders and the swing traders. Both groups have a similar goal of making profits from short term or long term trades. However, there are major differences between the two that you should understand and make your decision on your best choice depending on your level of technical expertise, time frames, and your preference.

Basically, day trading is a form of trading where your long or short position is entered and exited on the same day- opens and closes within 24hours. Day traders get into positions based on quantitative, fundamental, or technical reasons. Day traders do not hold their positions overnight. Swing trading, on the other hand, is a long term investment where the trader buys or shorts securities and holds them for some days, weeks, or months. Unlike day traders, the swing traders do not intend to take trading as a full-time job.

Also, you do not need to have lots of capital to swing trade, while day trading follows the '**pattern day trader rule.**' This rule is what governs any trader that makes more than four trades in the same security over five business days. This trader is referred to as "pattern day trader" based on the premise that the trades represent above 6% of the trader's total trading activity in that period. A pattern day trader must also have a minimum of $25,000 equity in their account on any trading day.

Day trading

Being a day trader can be very beneficial; however, it has its inherent risks. A day trader needs to realize that there may be times where he may encounter a 100% loss.

Day trading, more than some other type of trading, requires quick and right choices on positions and estimating the entry, exits, and stop-losses. The trades are fast and must be amazingly precise. Day trading imperatively requires being available and comprehending whatever occurs in the market at every point in time. Even though it doesn't imply that one should trade every day or consistently, the evaluations need to be done frequently. This type of trading takes more time than swing trading. However, it can be satisfying all-day work.

Day trading is better for people who have a passion for full-time trading and possess discipline, decisiveness, and diligence. For one to be successful as a day trader, he needs to have an in-depth understanding of charts and technical trading. Day trading can be stressful and intense, and so, traders need to be able to control their emotions and stay calm under fire.

Swing trading

A swing trader identifies swings in currencies, commodities, and stocks that occur over days. Unlike day trading, a swing trade may take up to weeks to work out. Swing traders have more persistence concerning their trade opening. As the positions extend to the second day, there is potential for huge benefits on a single trade, yet there are fewer trading opens generally. Anyone who has the investment capital and knowledge can give a shot at swing trading.

Swing trading requires less technical investigative abilities and progressively focus research and information on macroeconomics. The entry focus does not need to be that exact, and the planning isn't so pivotal since the moves which swing traders are expecting to get are bigger.

Swing trading doesn't require the trader to put in much time as frequent technical evaluation and consistent sitting before the screen is not necessary. It is usually a stress-free and low-effort job. The swing trader can have a separate full-time job as he does not have to stay glued to his computer screen all day.

Swing trades usually require time to work out. The more time a trade is open for days or week, the more the chances of having higher profits than trading multiple times daily on the same security. Margin requirements in a swing trade are higher since positions are held overnight. Compared to day trading whose maximum leverage is four times one's capital, swing trading is often two times the trader's capital.

Be that as it may, traders need to understand and utilize stop-losses and target levels to their benefit. While there is the possibility that the stop order will execute at an unfavorable price, it is still better than having to monitor all your open positions constantly.

As is normal with all types of trading, a swing trader can also experience losses, and because the traders hold the positions for a longer time, they may experience greater loss than the day traders.

Swing trading does not require the use of state of the art technology. You can swing trade with one computer, and any needed trading tools.

Because swing trading is usually not a full-time job, the traders have other sources of income and have reduced chances of burnout caused by stress.

When should you go for day trading?

The points below have summarized the ideal situation for you to be a day trader:

- You are disciplined, diligent, and strong-willed.
- You are willing to make small profits daily by making small trades.

- You have the minimum capital requirements stated by FINRA rules for pattern day traders and SEC, if and when they apply to you.
- You are knowledgeable and have the expertise to make great profits.
- You are not easily stressed, and you can manage stress.
- You are committed to studying current trends and can take needed action at the speed of light.
- You never have a dull day, and you are out for excitement every minute.

When should you go for swing trading?

The points below have summarized the ideal situation for you to be a swing trader:

- You lack extreme levels of technical understanding
- You do not want to go full time into trading. That is, you don't desire trading as your only source of income.
- You do not like stress and will instead go for something that is not as risky as day trading.

- You do not fancy constant monitoring of market activities.
- You are patient and can wait for weeks to months while studying the movements of the market.
- You have a full-time job and can't spare time for day trading activities.
- You do not have plenty of money to invest.

Retail Traders vs Institutional Traders

Trading securities can be as easy as hitting the buy or sell button on a computerized trading account. However, sophisticated traders will prefer to go for more complex trades that require setting a limit price on a block trade, traded over several days, and parsed over several brokers. The difference depends on the type of trader, and there are two basic types of traders: institutional trader and retail trader.

Retail traders, also known as individual traders, trade for themselves alone; that is, they buy or sell securities for personal accounts. Institutional traders, on the other hand, buy and sell securities for accounts that belong to a group or institution. Some common examples of institutional traders are mutual fund companies, pension funds, exchange-traded funds (EFTs), and insurance companies. These institutional traders trade on behalf of another party or persons.

In the past, institutional traders enjoyed more advantages than retail traders. However, the gap between the individual and institutional traders has reduced as both the institutional traders and retail traders now have access to sophisticated online brokerages, real-time data, the ability to trade in multiple securities, and availability of investment data and analysis.

Still, there are some advantages that the institutional traders have over the retail traders, which we will look at in this section along with the difference between the two types of traders.

Institutional Traders

These traders can invest in securities that are not available to retail traders like swaps and forwards. The type of transactions, as well as the complex nature of these transactions, usually prohibit or discourage individual traders.

Generally, institutional traders trade blocks of a minimum of 10,000 shares and can cut costs by sending trades through an intermediary or directly to the exchanges. These traders negotiate the basis point fees for every individual transaction, and they usually get the best price and execution. They do not get charged for marketing or distribution expense ratios.

Institutional traders can significantly influence the share price of securities due to the large volume of transactions that they handle. Because of this, they sometimes have to split their trades across various brokers or spread transactions over time in a bid to avoid making any material impact.

The larger the fund of an institution, the higher the market cap of that institutional trader. It is usually harder for these institutional traders to invest lots of cash in smaller cap stocks because they may not want to reduce the liquidity of a trade to the point that it will be hard for anyone to take the other side of the trade, neither will they want to be majority owners.

Institutional traders pay to have the fastest news feeds available on the market. They do this to get the market trending news and information faster than their competitors as some of the best trading opportunities happen right around these news events.

Institutional traders also concentrate squarely on developing and maintaining healthy trading psychology that keeps them focused on the matters that are most important in their trading activities. In fact, many organizations pay to have in-house psychologists that keep their traders mentally sharp and focused.

Institutional traders dwell on basics and emotions alongside an undiluted concentration on risk management, thus maintaining good trading psychology. Retail traders center on technical systems, price behaviors, and indicators while lacking proper risk management and trading psychology. Institutional traders greatly focus on how to manage risk, and once in a while, use leverage. Peradventure they utilize leverage, they are extremely cautious about not risking more percentage on that specific trade than they would if they had not utilized any leverage whatsoever. Should institutional traders leverage so much and screw up, they are liable to get fired. Institutional traders are typically reinforced with enough capital and get even more capital as they continue to show reliability and promote their track record.

Retail Traders

Typically, retail traders invest in options, bonds, futures, and stocks, and they have reduced or no access to IPOs. Most trades done by retail traders are in round lots, that is, 100 shares, but they can trade any amount of shares they want at a time. The cost of trading is higher for retail traders as they need to go through a broker who usually charges a flat fee for every trade, including charges for marketing and distribution.

The retail traders are also not able to influence the price of a security as they trade a fewer number of shares compared to the institutional traders.

While institutional traders do not like to go for small-cap stocks, retail traders are more likely to invest in these small-cap stocks, because the lower price points of these stocks allow these individual traders to buy several securities in several shares to give them a diversified portfolio.

The retail trader typically starts and closes up their trading practice using technical indicators. These indicators only predict future price movement through past price actions. This is not the same with the institutional traders as they do not need to use any kind of technical indicators to gain an edge in their trading.

Chapter 4: Choosing the Right Stocks to Trade

There are thousands of equities available for a trader to choose from, and day traders have no limit on the type of stocks they can trade; you can trade on virtually any stock of your choice. With all these available choices, it may seem like a difficult task to know the right stock to add to your watchlist. This takes us to the first step in day trading, which is knowing what to trade.

Here are some tips that will help you to choose the best stocks for maximum profits:

1. High Volatility and Liquidity in Day Trading

Liquidity in financial markets refers to how one can quickly buy or sell an asset in the market. It can also mean the impact that trading has on the price of a security. It is easier to day trade liquid stocks than other stocks; they are also more discounted, which makes them cheaper.

Liquid stocks are bigger in volume, in the sense that one can purchase and sell larger quantities of stock without having any significant effect on the price. Because day trading strategies depend on accurate timing and speed, a lot of volume makes it easier for traders to get in and out of trades. Depth is also important as it shows you the level of liquidity of stocks at different price levels below or above the current market offer and bid.

Also, corporations with higher market capitalizations have more liquid equities than those with lower market caps because it is easier to find sellers and buyers for stocks owned by these big corporations.

Stocks that have more volatility also follow the day trading strategies. A stock is considered volatile if the corporation that owns it experiences more adjustment in its cash flow. Uncertainty in the financial market creates a big opportunity for day trading. Online financial services like Google Finance or Yahoo Finance regularly list highly volatile and liquid stocks during the day. This information is also available on other online broker sites.

2. Consider Your Own Position

The stocks you decide to go for have to align with your goals and personal situation because there is no one-size-fits-all in the financial market. You have to put into consideration your capital, your risk appetite, and the type of investing you are going to take on. Let's not forget the role of research in all these. Your best bet is to read up on financials of different companies, study the market, consider the sectors that best reflect your values, personality, and personal needs, and remember to begin early. You need to be familiar with the market openings and time yourself to follow these openings. While day trading, ensure not to get emotionally attached to a particular stock. Don't forget that you are looking at patterns to know when best to exit or enter to minimize your losses and increase your profit. While you do not have to stay glued to your screen, you still need to know the earning season and what the economic calendar looks like. This will help you to pick the best stocks for day trading.

3. Social Media

This industry is also another attractive target for day trading as there are several online media companies like Facebook and LinkedIn, that have high trading volume for their stocks.

Also, there have been several debates on the capability of these social media companies to convert their massive user bases into a sustainable income stream. Although stock prices, in theory, represent the discounted cash flow of the companies that issued them, the recent valuations also look at the earning potential of these companies. Based on this, some analysts think that this has led to higher stock valuation than is suggested by the fundamentals. Regardless, social media is still a popular stock for day trading.

4. Financial Services

Financial services industries also offer great stocks for day trading. For example, Bank of America is one of the most highly traded stocks per trading session. If you are looking for company stock to day trade, stocks from Bank of America should be among your top consideration, despite the increased skepticism that the banking system is facing. The trading volume for Bank of America is high, which makes it a liquid stock. This also applies to Morgan Stanley, Citigroup, JP Morgan & Chase, and Well Fargo. They all have uncertain industrial conditions and high trading volumes.

5. Going Outside Your Geographical Boundary

When trading in the financial market, you must diversify your portfolio. Look at stocks listed in other exchanges like the London Stock Exchange (LSE) or Hong Kong's Hang Seng. Extending your portfolio outside your boundary will grant you access to potentially cheaper alternatives as well as foreign stocks.

6. Medium to high instability

A day trader needs to understand the price movement to be able to make money. As a day trader, you can choose to go for stocks that typically move a lot in percentage terms or dollar terms, as these two terms usually yield different results. Stocks that typically move 3% and above every day have a consistently large intraday moves to trade. This also applies to stocks that move above $1.50 each day.

7. Group followers

Although some traders specialize in contrarian plays, most traders will rather go for equities that move in line with their index and sector group. What this means is that, when the sector or index ticks upward, the price of individual stocks will also increase. This is crucial if the trader desires to trade the weakest or strongest stocks every day. If a trader will rather go for the same stock every day, then it is advisable to focus on that stock and worry less on whether it corresponds with any other thing.

Entry and Exit Strategies

After you must have picked the best stocks in the world, your strategies will determine if you will profit from them or not. There are several available day trading strategies, but to increase your chances of success, you need to stick to certain guidelines and look out for certain intraday trading signals.

Below, I will talk about 5 of these guidelines:

1. **Trade Weak Stocks in a Downtrend and Strong Stocks in an Uptrend**

Most traders, in a bid to pick the best stocks for day trading, prefer to look at EFTs or equities that have at least a moderate to high connection with the Nasdaq or S&P 500 indexes, and then separate the strong stocks from the weak ones. This creates an opportunity for the day trader to make profit as the strong stock has the potential to go 2% up when the index moves 1% up. The more a stock moves, the more opportunity for the day trader.

As market futures/ indexes move higher, traders should purchase stocks that have more aggressive upward movement than the futures. With this, even if the futures pull back, it will have little or no impact/ pull back on a strong stock. These are the stocks you should trade in an uptrend as they provide more profit potential when the market goes higher.

When the futures or indexes drop, it becomes profitable to short sell those stocks that drop more than the market. The ETFs and stocks that are weaker or stronger than the market may change each day, however, certain sectors may be relatively weak or strong for weeks at a time. When looking for a stock to trade, always go for the strongr one. This same rule applies to short trades as well. As a short seller, you should isolate EFTs or stocks that are weaker so that when prices fall, you will have greater chances of having profits by being in EFTs or stocks that fall the most.

2. Trade Only with the current intraday Trend

The trading market always moves in waves, and its your job as a trader to ride these waves. When there is an uptrend, your focus should be on taking long positions while you should focus on taking short positions whenever there is a downtrend. We have already established that intraday trends do not go on forever but, you can carry out one or more trades before a reversal occurs. When there is a shift with the dominant trend, you should begin to trade with the new trend. It may be difficult to isolate the trend, but you can find simple and useful entry and stop loss strategies from Trendlines.

3. Take your time. Wait for the Pullback

Trendlines provide visual guides that show where price waves will start and end. So, when choosing stocks to day trade, you can use a trendline for early entry into the next price wave. When you want to enter a long position, be patient and wait for the price to move down towards the trendline and then move back higher before you buy. Before an upward trendline can appear, a price low before a higher price low needs to happen. A line is drawn to connect the two points and then extends to the right. This same principle applies when short selling. Be patient for the price to move up to the downward-slope trendline, and once the stock starts to move back down, you can then make your entry.

4. Take your profits regularly

As a day trader, you have limited time to make profits, and for this reason, you need to spend very little time in trades that are moving in the wrong direction or losing money. Let me show you two simple guidelines that you can use to take profits when trading with trends:

- In a short position or downtrend, take your profits slightly below or at the former price low in the current trend.
- In a long position or uptrend, take your profits at slightly above or at the former price high in the current trend.

5. Do not play when the market stalls

The market may not always trend. The intraday trends may reverse so often that it becomes hard to establish an overriding direction. If there are no major lows and highs, ensure the intraday movements are large enough to increase the chances of profits and reduce the risks of lose. For instance, if you are risking $0.15 per share, the

EFT or stock should move enough to give you a minimum of $0.20 - $0.25 profit using the guidelines stated above. When the price is not trending (that is, moving in a range), move to a range-bound trading technique. During a range, you will no longer have an angled line, but rather a horizontal line. However, the general concept still applies: purchase only when the price goes to the lower horizontal area (support) and then begins to move higher. Short sell once you notice that the price has reached the upper horizontal line (resistance) and begins to go lower again.

Your buying strategy should be to exit close to the top of the range but not exactly at the top. Your shorting strategy should be to exit in the lower part of the range but not exactly at the bottom. The chances of making gains should be more than the risk of loss. Place a stop loss just above the most current high before entry on a short signal or just below the most current low before entry on a buy signal.

Several traders find it hard to alternate between range trading and trend trading and so they opt to do one or the other. If you choose to go for range trading, then you should avoid trading during trends, but focus on trading EFTs or stocks that tend to range. If trend trading on the other hand, avoid trading when the markets are ranging, and you should concentrate on trading EFTs or stocks that have the potential to trend.

Buying long. Selling short

Notwithstanding the nature of a stock, as soon as the value changes, some traders will be in profit while others will lose. Our major reason for trading stocks is to purchase while the value is low and sell when the value is high. However, several financial experts do the reverse- they first sell high then buy low. The term, long and short in stock market trading, refers to whether a trader initiated a trade by selling first or buying first. To initiate a short trade, the trader sells first before buying, with the intention to repurchase the stock at a reduced price and make some profit. Long trade, on the other hand, is initiated by buying stock to sell it at a higher price in the future and make a profit.

Long Trades/ Buying Long

In day trading, the term "long" and "buy" are used interchangeably. Except you're an incessant worrywart, buying a stock with the expectations that its offer cost will appreciate, is a decent way to invest in the market. Moreover, stocks have the best return of all significant assets, rounding up to about 8% to 17%, depending on the time of research. When a day trader goes long in a trade, it means that he or she bought an asset waiting to resell when the price goes up. The chances that the investment will yield some returns are very high, and financial experts also support the fact that buying today and staying on the sideline until there's an increase in price is a good decision. Subsequently, a whole lot of speculators purchase long in stocks and plan to get a decent return over a long period.

Application: Buying Long

For instance, let's assume as a trader, you bought 1000 shares of ABC stock for $20 per share and decide to go long, the transaction costs you $20,000. Then you get to sell the shares at $20.20 per share; your trading account gets funded with $20, 200 with a profit of $200 minus commissions. This is the desired result when a trader goes long. When you go long on a trade, you have unlimited profit potential since the price of an asset can increase indefinitely. A stock you purchased at $1, have the potential to rise as high as $150, $100, etc.

However, there is the possibility that the price may decrease. If you sell the shares above at $19.50, you will receive $19,500 for a trade of $20,000. You lose $500 plus the cost of commission.

The largest loss you may encounter in this trade is if the share value drops to $0, which is a $20 loss per share. However, day traders try to reduce risks and increase profits by entering into several small moves to avoid large price drops.

Selling Short/ Short Trades

This term may be confusing to most new traders as we all know that you can only sell what is in your possession. Simply put, the financial market allows you to sell first before buying back to replace the sold stock or buy first before selling.

In day trading, the term "short" and "sell" are used interchangeably. The term 'short' refers to an open position. For example, if a trader says, "I am short SPY," it means the trader currently has a short position in S and P 500 EFT. Traders often use the term "go short" or "going short" to indicate their desire to short a particular asset, that is, selling what they do not have.

In short selling, a trader opens a position by borrowing shares or other assets that the trader believes will decrease in value at an agreed future date, that is, the expiry date. The trader then sells these borrowed shares to any buyer that is willing to pay the market price. The trader is betting that before the expiry date for the borrowed asset, the price will crash, and then they can buy at a reduced cost. There is a high risk of loss on this type of trade as the price of an asset can rise to infinity.

If they can buy back at a price lower than their sell price, they realize a profit but if the reverse is the case, that is, they buy back the asset at a higher price than their sell price, they make some loss.

Application: Selling Short

Similar to the example above, you decide to go short on 1000 shares of ABC stock at $20 per share, your account gets credited with $20,000, which isn't your money yet. Your account will go into a negative of 1,000 shares, and some time in the future, you will need to return the account to zero by buying back a minimum of 1,000 shares. After you regularize your account, then you can tell if you made a profit or a loss. If you can repurchase the shares at $19.50, you will pay $19,500 for the 1,000 shares. This will give you a profit of $500 minus commission. However, if the price of the stock increases and you repurchase for $20.50 per share, you get charged $20,500 and you lose $500 plus commissions.

Chapter 5: Risk Management

Risk management can be considered as the one-percent rule used by traders to restrict huge losses to the barest minimum. As long as you manage the risk, you have a high chance of making huge profits in the foreign exchange market. Essentially, risk management is just a way of managing a trader's exposure to risks during buying and selling. Risk management helps to reduce your losses as well as protect a trading account from losing all the money invested.

Risk management is an important prerequisite to a successful day trading activity. However, it is often overlooked by several traders. After all, it is easy for a trader who has accumulated good profit to lose everything just in one or more bad trades if he has no proper risk management technique.

In this chapter, we will talk about some simple techniques that you can use to safeguard your trading profits:

1. **Plan your trades**

Sun Tzu, a Chinese military general, once said that "Every battle is won before it is fought." This means that it is the planning and strategy and not the war itself, that guarantees a win. In the same vein, a popular quote amongst successful traders is "Plan the trade and trade the plan." Planning ahead is a great determinant of if a trade will be successful or not.

The first step is to ensure that you are using a broker that handles frequent trading as some brokers are specifically for people who do not trade frequently. While their commissions are usually high, yet they do not have the right analytical tools that active traders need.

Two key ways that traders can plan ahead during a trade is the "Take Profit" and "Stop-Loss" points. A successful trader already knows his buy and sell prices. He or she then measure the subsequent returns against the possibility of the stocks hitting their goals. Once they are convinced that the adjusted return is high enough, they execute the trade.

Unsuccessful traders, on the other hand, usually go into a trade without any idea of the points they should sell at for profit or loss. When these traders suffer loss, they tend to hold on with the hope of making their money back. When they are in profit, they also hold on with the hope of making more gains.

2. **The One-percent rule**

Most day traders follow what is known as the one percent rule. This rule advises traders never to put more than one percent of their trading account or capital into a single trade. For instance, if you have $11,000 in your trading account, you should not invest more than $110 in any given instrument.

This technique is popular amongst traders that have $100,000 or less in their trading account; some traders even increase to 2% so long as they can afford it. Other traders with higher balances usually prefer to go for less than 1 percent because when the account size increases, the position also increases. The best way you can reduce your risk is to avoid going above the one percent rule.

Example of One Percent Rule

Say you have $10,000 in your trading account, it, therefore, means either of the following:

- No investment should have more than one percent of your account value, including borrowed money. This means that you have to limit your position to $100 of forex, stock, or any other instrument you wish to trade

OR

- You can employ leverages in such a way that the investments can go above $100 in value, but you will place a stop-loss on the trade to ensure that the monetary loss does not exceed $100.

   For example, if you take a $400 position, your stop-loss should never go above a 25% drop in market value (25% times $400 = $100), or whatever value equal to one percent of the value of your account.

How to Apply the One Percent Rule

The take-profit and stop-loss levels help you to calculate how you can apply the 1% rule ahead of time.

For instance:

A particular stock is trading at $10.00, and you wish to go long for that stock at $9.90. Your stop-loss is $9.85 while the take profit level is $10.05. You have $10,000 in your account. Now, how many shares of this particular stock can you buy to maintain the 1% rule?

You need first to know how much you can lose on any trade:

$10,000 * 1% = $100

The maximum loss per share is the difference between your buy price and your stop-loss. In this example, the difference is $0.05, that is, $9.90 - $9.85.

Now, take your maximum loss amount, then divide by the maximum loss for each share:

$100/ $0.05/ share = 2,000 shares.

So, if your broker allows you to buy up to this amount, you can go ahead to buy 2,000 shares of the desired stock.

3. Set Stop-Loss and Take-Profit Points

Stop loss is the price you are willing to sell a stock at a loss. This usually occurs when a trade does not go the way the trader expected. The stop-loss point is created to avoid the mentality that the price will come back up and limit losses before it gets worse. For instance, if a stock goes below a key support level, most traders will sell as soon as possible.

The take-profit point, on the other hand, is the price the trader is willing to sell a stock and take profit. For instance, when a stock approaches a key resistance level after hitting a large upward move, traders may wish to sell the stocks before consolidation happens.

How to Set Stop-Loss Points

While traders use technical analysis to set stop-loss and take-profit points, fundamental analysis is also important. For instance, a trader buys a stock ahead of earning, and as excitement builds, she or he may decide to sell the stock before the news gets to the market, not minding that the take-profit target is yet to hit, especially if expectations have become extremely high.

The most popular way of setting these points is by 'moving averages' as the market widely tracks these averages, and they are also easy to calculate. The major moving averages are 9-, 5-, 50-, 20-, 200- and 100-day averages. The best way to set these averages is by applying them to a chart of a stock and then determining if the stock price has reacted to them previously at either resistance or support level.

Another way you can place the take-profit or stop-loss levels is on resistance or support trend lines. To draw these lines, simply connect previous lows or highs that happened on significant, above average volume. Similar to the moving averages, the major factor is determining the levels at which the price reacted to the trend lines as well, on high volume.

Here are some major considerations when setting these points:

- Use known fundamental events like earning releases, as the major time or period to go in or out of a trade as uncertainty and volatility can rise.

- Modify your stop loss following the market's volatility. Tighten the stop-loss points if the stock price isn't moving well.

- Use longer-term moving averages for stocks that are more volatile to reduce the possibility that a meaningless price swing will trigger the execution of the stop-loss order.

- Stop-losses should be at least 1.5 times the current high-to-low range to avoid it being executed for no reason.

- Regulate the moving averages to match the ranges of the target price. For instance, longer targets need to use larger moving averages to reduce the number of signals generated.

4. Calculate expected returns

Setting take-profit and stop-loss points will also help to calculate the expected return. This calculation is very important as it makes traders reflect on their trades and justify their reasons for any trade actions they take. It also gives traders a systematic way of comparing several trades and choosing the most profitable.

Use the formula below to get the calculation:

[(Possibility of Gain) x (Take Profit percentage Gain)] + [(Possibility of Loss) x (Stop-Loss percentage Loss)]

Whatever result you get from this calculation is the expected return for active traders. The trader then measures the result against other opportunities to decide which stocks to trade. The possibility of loss or gain can be calculated using historical breakdowns and breakouts from the resistance or support levels, while experienced traders can make an informed guess.

5. Diversify

To make the most out of your trading, you must never have all your eggs in one basket. When you invest all your money in one instrument or stock, you increase your risk of having big losses. You need to diversify across the geographic regions and in all sectors of the industry. This will not only help you manage your risk but will also give you access to more viable opportunities.

6. **Downside Put Options**

If you are permitted to do options trading, you can buy a downside **"Put Option,"** also called protective put, to serve as a hedge against losses from trades gone bad. With the put option, you have the right, though not under obligation, to sell an underlying stock at a stated price before or as the option expires. For example, you own ABC stocks from 100 dollars, and you buy the 6-month $90 Put for $2 per option in premium. You will automatically be stopped out from the trade if the price drops below $88 ($90 strike minus the $2 premium paid).

Trading Psychology

Trading psychology refers to the mental state and emotions of a trader, which can dictate the failure or success in trading securities. This concept represents the several aspects of one's behaviors and characters that can influence the actions taken during a trade. It is as important as other attributes like skill, experience, and knowledge when it comes to trade success.

The two most critical aspects of trading psychology are risk-taking and discipline, as the implementation of these two aspects plays a crucial role in the success of a trader's trading plan. Greed and fear are two common emotions that drive trading behavior, along with regret and hope.

Understanding Trading Psychology

The term 'Trading Psychology' is associated with certain behaviors that can make or mar a trade. Severally, the emotionally-driven behavior of traders is due to either fear or greed. Greed is the excessive desire for riches that can cloud a trader's judgement and rationality if not watched as trades inspired by greed often cause traders to display several behaviors during a trade. These behaviors include buying shares from a company or technology that is not yet tested simply because the price is rapidly going up, making high-risk trades, or buying shares without making any research on the investment. Also, greed is another reason traders stay in profitable trades longer than they should, with the hope of getting more profit or expanding their positions. We see greed play out mostly in the last phase of bull markets, especially amidst several speculations, the careless investors then throw caution to the wind.

Fear, on the other hand, causes traders not to take risks due to concerns of large losses or prematurely closing out on positions. Fear is commonly seen during the bear market and can cause traders to make irrational decisions in their haste to leave the market. Fear often causes traders to panic and lead to several panic selling.

Regret can make traders who missed the initial rise of a stock to invest in that stock at its peak point. This violates all trading discipline and often leads to massive losses from prices that crash from their high peaks.

Technical Analysis

Technical analysts who rely on charting to drive their trade decisions need to understand trading psychology; security charting provides a broad display of insight on the movement of a security. Charting techniques and technical analysis help the trader to spot trends for buying and selling opportunities, but the trader also needs to understand and follows his instinct for market movements, which can be derived from the trading psychology of the trader.

There are several cases in technical charting where traders need to rely on the chart's insight as well as their knowledge of the stocks they are following and their instincts for the effects of broader factors on the market. Traders that pay keen attention to confidence, displine, and comprehensive security price influences, display balance trading psychology that leads to greater success.

Importance of Trading Psychology

While there are several skills that a trader needs to have to be successful in the financial market, yet none of these skills are as important as the mindset of the trader. Day trading requires the trader to think fast and make decisions quickly, entrying, and exiting trades on short notice. To be successful in this, the trader needs to be disciplined and avoid emotions.

Understand Fear

It is normal to be scared when we hear bad news about the market or a particular stock. Traders may overreact and feel the need to liquidate their investment or stop themselves from taking any risks. When this happens, they may succeed in avoiding some losses but may also miss out on great gains. Every trader needs to understand that fear is a natural reaction, and as a trader, you need to stop for a moment to ponder on what your fears are as well as the reason for the fear. When you ponder on these issues before time and conscious of your response to some things, it then makes it easy for you to isolate and identify those feelings during a trading session and focus on how to get past the emotion. While it may not be easy to achieve and requires practice, it is also important if you want to succeed.

Overcome Greed

It is not easy to overcome greed, as it is usually based on one's desire to do better or achieve more. Traders should be able to recognize this emotion and only build trading plans that are void of emotions and harmful instincts.

Set Rules

Traders need to set rules that guide them in entrying or exiting a trade, based on their tolerance for risk-rewards – be it through stop-loss or profit target. This way, emotions will be completely out of the equation. Traders also need to set limits on the amount they wish to win or lose for each day. Once your profit target is met, take the money and exit. Also, when the trade hits your set loss, exit the trade to prevent further loss.

Research and Review

Traders need to do extensive research about their area of interest: educate yourself, go for trading seminars, and attend sell-side conferences. It is also important for traders to devote the needed time to do researches; this includes reading trade journals, speaking with management, studying charts as well as other background searches to ensure that you are well prepared for the trading sessions. A knowledgeable trader will be able to conquer fear.

Also, traders need to be flexible and willing to experiment with new stocks periodically. One of the best ways to learn as a trader is by experimenting. The lessons you will learn from the experiments will help to reduce emotional influences.

Lastly, traders need to assess their performance periodically. Apart from reviewing their individual positions and returns, traders should reflect on how current they are on the market, how well prepared they are for a trading session, their progress in educating themselves, and so much more. These assessments will help the trader to change bad habits and correct identified mistakes, which will, in turn, improve the trader's overall returns.

Chapter 6: Introduction to Candlestick

Daily candlestick, just like bar charts, shows the market's low, high, close, and open prices for each trading day. Day traders use the candlesticks to make decisions on their trades based on patterns that occur regularly, forecasting the short-term movement of price.

In a candlestick, there is the body that shows the price range between the open and close for a particular day's trading and the wick or shadow that shows the low prices and high prices of a particular day's trading.

Candlestick offers information to traders about price actions and the emotions of the market toward a certain stock or security. For instance, bullish candles are formed when a stock-open moves 'low', tests support, and then springs back to close at a 'high.' Traders study the candlesticks to know which stocks are more promising to trade.

In the subsequent section, we will talk about the different kinds of candlestick patterns and how they can be used to predict market movement.

Bullish candlesticks

A bullish candlestick has a higher closing price than its opening price. Bullish candlestick patterns have an upward trend on the candlestick, usually green or white. Note that several candlesticks may form a pattern that includes one or more bearish candlesticks.

Below are the commonly used bullish candlestick patterns in day trading:

Hammer Candlestick

The hammer candlestick has a short body with an extended wick at the lower part of the body and usually forms at the bottom of a downward trend to indicate a near-term price bottom.

A hammer suggests that although there were selling pressures at some point of the day, ultimately, a strong buying pressure drove the rates up again. While the color of the whole body may differ for the hammer candlestick, the green hammers imply a stronger bull market than red hammers. I will advise that you make use of momentum indicators like RSI, stochastic etc. to time your entry. The best time to enter is when the

hammer with a trail stop either below the low of the hammer candle or the body low.

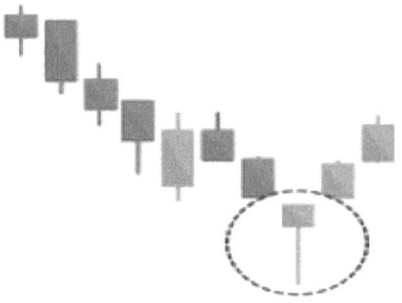

Inverted Hammer

Another bullish pattern is the inverted hammer. This pattern is like the upside down version of the hammer pattern. The only distinction is that the upper wick appears longer, while the lower wick appears shorter. You see this pattern after a downtrend as a sign of a trend-reversal.

It shows a buying pressure and a selling pressure that was not strong enough to pull the market price down. The inverted hammer depicts that buyers will soon have control over the market.

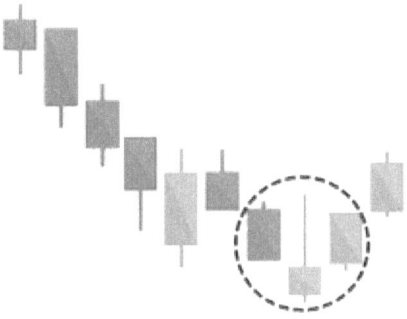

Bullish engulfing

This candlestick appears when the buyers outdo the sellers. For this pattern, you will see two candlesticks: the first candle is a small red body that is engulfed by a long green cable. This shows that the second trading day opened lower than the first, and once the bulls take control, prices will likely go high, and traders will make more gain from the increase.

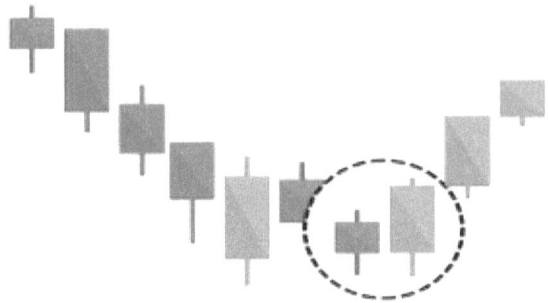

Piercing line

The piercing line is made up of two candlesticks, a long red candle, and a long green candle. There is usually a broad gap between the closing price of the red candlestick and the opening price of the green candlestick. It signifies a strong buying pressure, as the price is forced up to or at most, above the mid-price of the previous day.

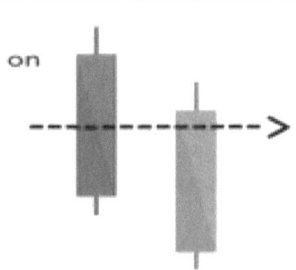

- A strong red body on the first bar
- The close on the second bar must be more than half-way up the body of the first bar.

Bearish Candlestick

A bearish candlestick depicts that the opening price is higher than the closing price. A bearish pattern comes with a downward trend. A bearish pattern doesn't point to the fact that every single candlestick is bearish as a lot depends on the timeframe of the candlestick. Below are the common bearish candlestick patterns in trading:

Hanging man

The hanging man looks a lot like the bullish hammer pattern. The only difference is the shape that forms at the end of an uptrend. It reveals that there was a huge sell-off during the day, but buyers were able to force the price up again. The significant sell-off is usually an indication that the bulls have lost control of the market.

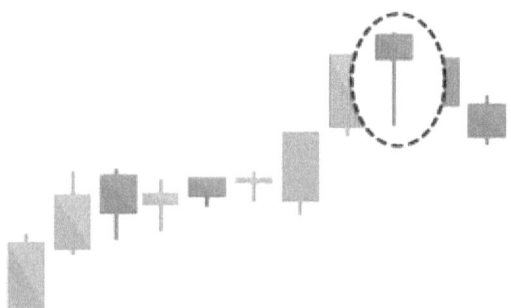

Shooting star

The shooting star looks a lot like the inverted hammer pattern, only that this is formed in an uptrend: it has a short lower body and a longer upper wick.

Usually, the market will gap a little bit higher on opening and rally to an intra-day high before it closes at a price above the open – in the form of a star falling from a height.

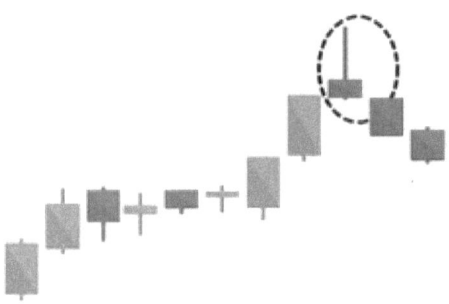

Bearish engulfing

A bearish engulfing pattern happens at the end of an uptrend. The first candle is a small green body that is engulfed by another long red candle. It shows a peak and then a reduction in price movement. It symbolizes an impending market downturn. The lower the second candle goes, the increase in the size of the trend.

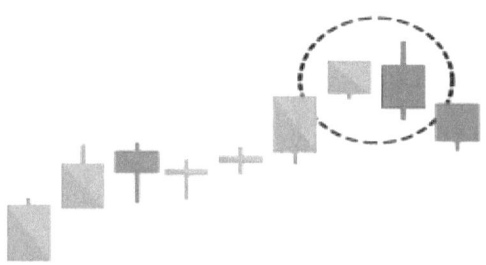

Evening star

The evening star has three candlesticks, just like the bullish morning star. It is a combination of a short candle sandwiched between a large red candle and a long green candlestick. It shows the reversal of an uptrend and is usually very strong when the third candlestick rubs off the top of the first candle.

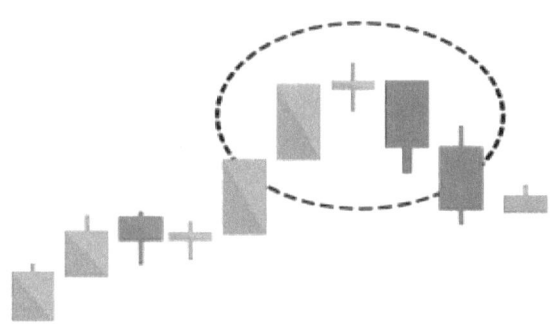

Indecision Candlesticks

Indecision candlestick patterns form within the market chart showing that both selling and buying pressures are balanced. This means that neither the bull nor the bear is in control of the market. We have two types of indecision pattern, which you will better understand as we move further.

The Spinning Top Pattern

Spinning top pattern is a type of indecision pattern which forms when both selling and buying pressure struggles to have control over the market. One way to identify a spinning top pattern candlestick is that the candle has a long upper and lower shadow. Another way you can tell a spinning top pattern is its small body, as seen in the diagram above.

The spinning top pattern shows two things: firstly, as soon as the market opens, both buyers and sellers aggressively want to take charge resulting in upper and lower shadows. Secondly, it shows that none of them gained at the end of the session.

Simply, the spinning top pattern shows huge volatility within the market without a clear outcome of who won between the buyers and the sellers.

The Doji Pattern

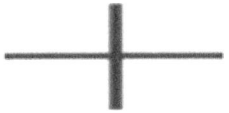

Doji pattern is another type of indecision pattern formed when both buying and selling pressure is balanced. You can identify this in two ways. Firstly, the open and close of the candle are somewhere in the middle of the range. Secondly, both the upper and lower shadows are short and about equal length.

Chapter 7: Setting up your Charts - Technical Indicators

A chart gives detailed information about a stock or data that a trader wishes to analyze. But do these charts actually help traders make investment decisions according to their unique strategy, risk constraints, objectives, and time horizon? Below, we'll discuss three tips you should consider when setting up your charts.

1. **Pick a time frame that matches your investment range**

Your chart is likely to have a default time frame when you first open the chart (e.g., six months or a year). The first thing to do is to adjust this default time to suit your preferred timing.

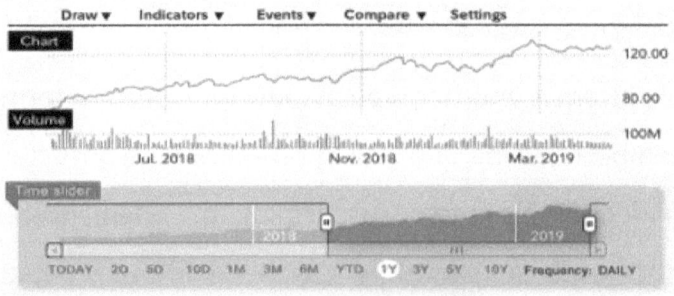

Choosing a time frame that fits your investment horizon is important—for a whole lot of reasons. Let's assume you are a longer-term investor with a 1-year to 10-years time horizon, viewing an intraday, or 1-week chart wouldn't be ideal. Instead, viewing a 5- or 10-year chart is more suitable to present you with a broader scope of the long-term trends that are closer fits to your investment time horizon. On the other hand, assuming you are thinking about a short-term momentum trade, a multi year chart might not be ideal.

One other reason that makes adjusting the time frame crucial is that the trends that may be obvious within the course of one session can appear much different when viewing within another time frame. For instance, a downtrend could be clear when viewing in a 1-month chart, but, if you were to adjust the time frame for the same chart to 1 year, the 1-month downtrend could appear more like a minor adjustment within a much longer-term bullish uptrend. The best bet is to look at different time frames to get a more holistic perspective.

2. Select the type of chart

The two common charts used by traders are the Line Charts and the Open-High-Low-Close Charts (OHLC charts). Open-high-low-close charts are also called bar charts. You can adjust the chart to display only the items you want to see (see sample in the chart below)

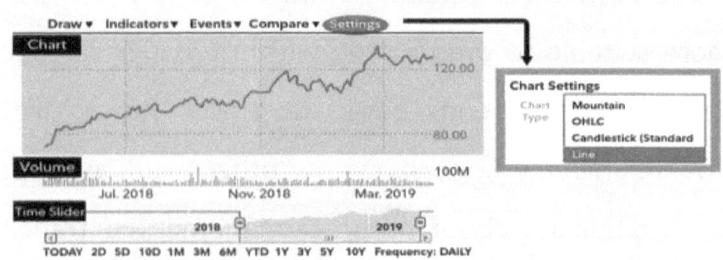

Each plot on an open-high-low-close chart reveals four price information. However, a line chart, which is the simulator type of chart—plots only the closing prices and links each plot with a line.

There are different trading platforms available, and each has its own setting menu. For some of these platforms, you can navigate to the setting menu, and change to a "mountain" or "candlestick" chart in addition to the open-high-low-close chart and line chart. A mountain chart is no different from a line chart, only that the portion under each plot is shaded to help reveal trends more clearly.

A candlestick chart, on the other hand, dramatically changes the view of a chart and is commonly used among some advanced chartists who are familiar with the analysis of candlestick patterns.

3. Add a Comparable Index and Technical Indicators

As soon as you have set your time frame and the type of chart you want, the next step is to add a comparable index or security to the chart.

For example, if you were reviewing a technology stock, it might be advisable to add the S&P 500® Index or a technology index to compare the stock with. This will give more comprehension about the performance of the stock by comparing its absolute strength with a comparable benchmark or stock.

Technical indicators are another component that you need to add to your stock, indicators like the Relative Strength Index (RSI), Moving Averages, or Moving Average Convergence-Divergence (MACD). These indicators will support in identifying trends that show if an asset is oversold or overbought. It will also help the trader to decide the ideal price level to trade.

Chapter 8: Supports and Resistance

Support and resistance levels are the horizontal price levels that unite price bar 'highs' to other price bars 'highs' or 'lows to lows,' thereby creating horizontal levels on a price chart.

The resistance or support level forms when a market's price action reverses and alters its direction, thereby leaving a trough (swing point) or peak in the market. Support and resistance levels can form trade ranges, as you will see in the chart below. They are also seen in trending markets as the market traces back, leaving behind trough/ swing points.

Trade price usually follows these support and resistance levels until the price is able to break through them.

The chart below is an example of support and resistance levels showing price within a trading range. A trading range happens when a security or stock trades between constant low and high prices for a while. The bottom of a trading range usually offers price support while the top provides price resistance.

In the chart below, you will notice that the price went off and out of the trading range, went above the resistance level before coming back down to test the old resistance level, it then maintained price and acted as support.

Support and resistance levels in a market can also form from swing points within a trend. As the market moves, it finds its way back on the trend, thereby leaving a 'swing point' in the market. This swing point looks like a trough in a downtrend, and like a peak in an uptrend.

When the price goes up, the previous peak serves as support after the price has gone up past them and then goes back down to test them. The opposite applies in a downtrend: the previous trough acts as resistance after the price has gone down through these levels and then finds its way back up to test them.

How To Trade Price Action Signals From Support and Resistance Levels

No trader can do without the Support and resistance levels as it helps to examine price action most comprehensively. Whenever price action entry signal forms at the main resistance or support level, it indicates a high-possibility entry point.

This main level then forms a 'barrier' that you can use to place your stop-loss beyond, and because there is a strong possibility that this will be a turning point in the trade, there's always a beneficial risk-reward ratio formed at main levels of resistance and support.

With the price action entry signal like the pin bar signal, you will see some confirmation that price will actually move from the major resistance or support level.

When you study the chart below, you will see that a bearish fakey strategy and a key resistance level formed at it. With the way the fakey strategy showed a false-break of the major resistance and an aggressive reversal, the price may continuously drop following the signal:

In the chart below, you will see that at times, a previous swing level in a trending market will act as a new level of support or resistance and help us to focus attention on price action entry signals.

In the example below, there was an uptrend, and the old swing high in the upward movement ended up as support level after the price went up above it. By the time the price returned to retest the level for the 2nd time, it had created a nice pin bar entry signals for traders to buy and re-enter the upward price movement from a confluent level.

Now let us look at the last chart in this section, which is quite interesting. Take a look at the swing low that formed on the left side of the chart during a downtrend. From the chart, it is evident how this level maintained relevance months later, not minding that the trend went from down to up. It started by acting as a resistance level but as soon as the resistance broke, we noticed an uptrend after which this same level acted as support, and this gave rise to the fakey pin bar combo signal seen in the chart:

Support and Resistance Tips

- You do not need to draw every little level on your charts but rather focus on finding the major daily chart levels, similar to what you see in the examples above. Those are the ones that matter.
- The horizonal resistance or support lines that you draw may not always touch the particular point

of low or high of the bars it connects. There is no problem if the line connects bars somewhat up from the low or down from the high. You need to understand that this is not science but rather a skill that you learn through constant practice, time, and experience.

- If you ever get confused about taking a particular price action entry signal, first identify if that is the key support or resistance level. If the answer is No, it is advisable not to take that signal.

- Price trading strategies like the inside bar, fakey, or pin bar strategy, will likely perform better if formed from confluent support or resistance level in a market.

Chapter 9: Order Types

Trading is somewhat more complex than just buying and selling. There are various ways you can buy and sell using different order types, and each order has its distinct function. With the growing awareness of the importance of the internet and digital technology, several investors now prefer to trade for themselves rather than pay large commissions to advisors to execute trades. But, before you can begin to buy and sell stocks, you need to know the different order types and when to use them.

In this chapter, we will cover the different types of stock orders and how you can apply them to your trades:

1. **A market order**

A market order, which is the most basic type of trade, is an order to buy or sell security instantly, irrespective of what the price is at the moment. This type of order gives assurance that the order will be applied but does not give assurance of the execution price. A market order generally will come to play at or near the present bid. So, if you want to buy a stock immediately, you will buy at a price that is close to or at the posted **Ask.** To sell a stock with this order type, you will be credited at a price that is close to or at the posted **Bid.**

However, traders need to know that market order may not be executed at the last traded price of that stock, especially in a volatile and fast moving market. The only time the price remains the same is if the bid and ask prices are exactly the same as the last traded price. This order type is popularly used by traders who need to sell or purchase a stock without any delays. One advantage of this order type is that you have the assurance that your trade order will be filled, infact, it will be done ASAP. And even if you can't tell the particular price for the execution, market orders on securities that trade above tens of thousands of shares each day are likely to execute close to the ask and bid prices.

2. **Limit order**

This type of order is also referred to as pending orders. It allows traders to buy and sell securities or stocks at a defined or better price in the future. This order type executes a trade only if the price hits the pre-set price if not, the order remains open. So, a limit order sets the minimum or maximum price you want to sell or buy a stock. For instance: An investor wants to buy shares of XYZ stock for not more than $20. The investor will fill a limit order for $20. In essence, the investor will not pay more than $20 for that stock, but he can buy the stock for less than $20.

We have four types of limit orders. Let us look at each below:

- **Sell Limit:** This is an order type set to sell a security or stock above or exactly at a specified price. To get the best price, you need to place the order above or at the current market ask.

- **Buy Limit:** This is an order to buy a stock below or exactly at a specified price. To get the best price, you need to place the order below or at the current market bid.

- **Sell stop:** this is an instruction to sell a stock at a price that is below the current market ask. This order type only gets filled once the trade gets to the pre-determined price level. Sell stop orders are placed below the market while the buy stops are placed above the market. Once a trade hits the stop level, it instantly converts into a limit order or market order. This type of order is used to exit long trades.

- **Buy stop order:** this is an instruction to purchase a stock at a price that is above the current market bid. Just like the sell stop, this order type only gets filled once the trade gets to the pre-determined price level. This order type is used as a stop-loss on short positions, particularly when the price is moving against you.

3. Stop-Loss Order

This is also known as an on-stop buy, on-stop sell, or stopped market. This order type is one of the most useful orders and differs from market order and limit orders. For this order type, the order stays dormant until it passes a certain price, then it gets activated as a market order. For example, if you place a stop-loss sell order on ABC shares at $50 per share, the order will remain dormant until the price gets to or goes below $50. It will then convert into a market order and then sell the shares at the best price in the market. This type of order is used for traders who do not have the luxury of time to monitor the market continually but want to protect themselves from massive downside move. The best time to apply this type of order is before you go on a vacation or long trips.

4. Stop-Limit Order

This order type is similar to the stop-loss orders, but for this type of order, there is a set limit on the price at which they should execute. The stop-limit order has two specified prices: the limit price and the stop price (the stop price converts the order to a sell order). Instead of the order to convert to a market order to sell, the sell order converts to a limit order, which will only execute when it hits the limit price or a better price.

5. All or None (AON)

This is popularly used by traders who purchase penny stocks. The order ensures that you get your complete order quantity or nothing at all. This becomes a problem if a limit is placed on the order or if the requested stock is not liquid. For instance, you place an order to purchase 1,000 shares of ABC, but the company is only selling 500 shares at the time. This type of order means that your request will not be filled until the available shares are up to 1000 and available at your set price. But if you did not place an all-or-none order, your order for 1,000 shares will partially be filled with 500 shares.

6. **Fill or Kill (FOK)**

This order type is a combination of the AON and the IOC (Immediate or cancel). This order commands that the whole order size be traded within a limited time, usually within seconds. The order gets cancelled if the condition is not met.

7. **Immediate or Cancel (ioc)**

This order commands that only the amount of an order that can be executed within a very short time, usually a few seconds, should be filled while the remaining of the order should be cancelled. If none of the shares is traded within the given interval, the trade gets cancelled totally.

8. **Take Profit**

This type of order is sometimes referred to as a profit target. The aim is to close out a trade at a profit after it has gotten to a specified level. Once the Take profit order is executed, the trade position closes. This order type is always linked to an open position of a pending order.

9. **Good Till Cancelled (GTC)**

This type of order places time restrictions on different orders. The orders stay active until you move to cancel them. For most brokerages, the maximum time you can leave an order active is 90 days.

10. **Day**

This order type is a follow up on the GTC, in the sense that, if you did not place an expiry date on the GTC instruction, the order automatically gets set to one day order. So, once the trading day is over, that particular order expires. You would have to re-enter the trade the next day if it did not get filled the previous day.

Level 2 Trading

Level 2 is a subscription based service that gives traders real-time access to the NASDAQ order book. In this NASDAQ order book, you will find price quotes for every price level, the size on each order as well as which market maker has what order. On the left side of the Level 2 window, you will find the bid prices and sizes while the right side shows the ask prices and sizes.

This service arms traders with detailed price information, including available prices as posted by electronic communication networks, and market makers. Electronic Communication Networks are computerized orders, and anyone can trade using the ECNs, even the big traders use this ECN. Market makers give the market its liquidity; however, they can mess with traders' stop losses. Market makers are obligated to buy and sell when no one else is doing so. Therefore, they determine the market in a way.

One thing you need to understand, though, is that not every order that disappears from the level 2 window is executed. Level 2 is an order book and so contains all the live orders in the market. Sellers and buyers can decide to pull out their orders at any time, which is why you will see orders disappear from the book.

Level 2 order book is very important, particularly for active trades that want to know where the interest of buyers and sellers is in the market.

While level 1 provides traders with needed information like best bid and ask prices, the level 2 goes further to display the supply and demand of the price levels outside the NBBO (National Best Bid Offer) price. The user gets to see visual display of price ranges and connected liquidity at each price level. Traders then use this information to determine entry and exit points that offers enough liquidity that a trader needs to complete the trade.

Benefits of the Level 2 Service

One major benefit of this service is that it offers access to rich information that concerns the market. A trader can maximize this information in several ways to make a profit. For instance, the window helps a trader to know the order sizes and liquidity volumes for stocks traded on NASDAQ. You can also identify trends by using data from the bid and ask orders.

The level 2 quotes also provide important data related to institutional investors and market makers that a trader can use to maximize his profit. For instance, you can know an institutional trader's interest in a large stock by looking at their order sizes, and then you place your identical orders. You can use this same strategy with reserve orders (these are large orders that are broken into smaller sizes.) After you have discovered hidden orders by looking at the Level 2 window, you can then place your identical order because when institutional traders invest in a stock, they help the resistance and support levels for the price of that stock.

Times and Sales

Time and sales or T&S are the most comprehensive representation of a market's trading information. The time and sales give real-time detail of individual trades done in the market. Plus, they present a variety of news about each trade (e.g., the exact time, the direction, the number of contracts traded, etc.). This is where graphical charts are used to give a summary of a market's price actions. This data is used for technical analysis. For instance, the T&S data will show that a buy order for 80 shares of ABC stock was made on the NASDAQ at 11:20:15 for $55.32.

The T&S will show you the information below for individual trade:

- **Date and Time:** The date and the specific time the trading occurred.
- **Direction:** Whether the trade was a buying or a selling transaction.
- **Price:** The price at which the trade happened.

- **Volume or Size:** The number of agreements (or shares, etc.) traded.

This data is usually accessed via the trading platform and is located in the time and sales window. In this window, you will see a running count of trades for the shares of a certain stock in a table format. You will find each of these main components of the T&S displayed in columns: date and time, volume, price and direction. The rows of data have its colors to identify trades that occurred in, on or outside the ask or bid. Several trading platorms permit trades to customize how these time and sales data are displayed.

How to Strategize using Time and Sales Data

Different traders have their own strategies and tools that they use to decide on stocks to buy and sell. Some use fundamental analysis to know the fundamental value of a share by looking at the financials of companies, while other traders use technical analysis to forecast prices by plugging trading volumes and price movements into statistical models. One of the technical analysis methods used by traders involves analyzing time and sales information.

Data obtained from T&S can be used alongside graphs and charts to estimate share price movement. For instance, candlestick charts and bar charts show trading ranges for specified timeline in aggregate and are used to see the double bottom, handle and Hikkake patterns. This gives a broad view of volume and price trends. If added to the details from the T&S data, a trader can get more details about the trend of an asset or stock.

Traders can also use the data from the T&S to decide if they want to execute a trade by themselves. However, new traders need to be conscious as the volume of data updates seen on the T&S window can put them off guard. As a new trader, first watch the price, volume and direction for a short time to understand how it works before you begin to use the data.

Hot Keys

Hotkeys are the shortcuts on your keyboard that can be entered to place buy and sell orders instantly. With the push of a button, you can have a buy or sell order in the market, saving you time and, often, countless dollars.

How to Set Up Hotkeys

Several online trading and particularly direct access trading platforms have the hot key functionality, usually in the settings field. So, you can buy and sell live market orders with the touch of two buttons.

Benefits of Hot Keys

Simply put, you're getting in and out of a trade just within the short time it takes you to press two keys on your keyboard- that's a rather quick trade. It usually takes a couple of clicks on a mouse and confirmation before initiating a trade. With hotkeys, it's done in no time. The first 15 minutes the market opens tends to be extremely volatile. Using the hotkey strategy helps you make profits during these volatile periods.

Although this function may seem hard at first, once you practice and get used to them, they become indispensable.

1. Faster cancels:

One convenient hotkey is the **"Cancel All Order"** button. For instance, you have five different buy-limit orders for five different stocks, then the price begins to fall hard, and you need to exit all limit orders quickly. Normally, you have to open each stock and then cancel the order.

But if you have a "Cancel All" key, you can cancel all the live orders by tapping just one key.

2. Speed

Another major benefit of the hotkey is speed. You will enjoy this more when you need to place multiple orders on different stocks. Also, you can set a hotkey to sell limit on the inside ask or buy limit on the inside bid with a set number of shares. This will not only save you time but will also save you lots of moving and pointing your mouse.

To ensure your trades are executed promptly, you need to have a good trading computer. A slow computer may not be well-suited with hotkey optimization. Be sure to have the best laptop for trading; it's worth the profit and convenience you'll get while trading. Even having something as simple as an adjustable standup desk can allow you to be fresh and ready to trade quickly. You are assured of trading at the speed of lightning if you are using hotkeys on a good PC.

Chapter 10: Trend Trading Strategies

Trend trading is a trading pattern that allows traders to collect gains by analyzing the movement of an asset in a particular direction. A trend is simply the movement of price in one direction, whether up or down. Trend traders go into long positions when an asset is trading upward, and they go into a short position when an asset begins to trend lower. Uptrends have higher swing highs and higher swing lows while downtrends have lower sing highs and lower sing lows.

Trend trading strategies believe that an asset will constantly move in the same direction as long as it is trending. This strategy is usually used by short term, long term, and intermediate term traders.

Some traders will purchase at point 1 (trend line support and Fibonacci retracement level) or 2 (a break of a "Flag" model). Some will wait for point 3 (a break over the former high). Of course, the lower you buy, the higher your profit can be.

Below are terms associated with the trend trading strategy:

Take profit: You can set your profit target at the previous high of the uptrend (or previous low of the downtrend) or even at levels beyond the previous uptrend and downtrend once you are confident in your trade.

Stop Loss: Note that when you are dealing with trend trading, you can use a tracking stop that accompanies the trend. This is because it may be difficult to know where to place your stop loss.

Scaling in: Trend trading allows you to add to your position, especially when you enter a trade as soon as the market begins to move, and your trade is successful. This will give you more chances of increasing your profit, but also remember to adjust your risk management as you add to your position. You can also start with less trade like buying at point 1, then raise your position as the price gets higher. This method will help to reduce your risks.

Trend Trading Indicators

Traders have come up with several ways to recognize these fundamental trends, which includes observing price action. But the most prevalent trend trading strategies use technical indicators. Popular trend trading indicators are as follows:

Moving average

Moving Average indicator is a broadly used indicator to reach a conclusion that is not based on one or two phases of price fluctuations. Moving averages give a sharp idea of whether to take a long or short position on an asset. If the stock describes a negative trend, that is, the price is beneath the moving average, take a short position (sell) on the stock. But, if the stock price is higher than the simple moving average, one should take a long position (buy) on the stock as there are high chances of the stock price growing further.

Relative strength index (RSI)

This is an oscillator that measures extreme emotion in a trending stock. The RSI is deemed to be one of the best complimentary indicators known for trend trading.

Once a stock hits 70 and above out of 100 on the RSI, it is said to be 'overbought' and possibly due for an adjustment. In the same vein, a stock is considered oversold when the RSI is less than 30. Several trend traders utilize the RSI to capture the last few stretches of a big trend. For instance, a stock with a strong trend and an RSI of 60 possibly has a little more way to go before closing or adjusting downward.

In a strong uptrend, the price can get to 70 and above and remain on that level for a long time, and the same applies to the downtrend.

On Balance Volume (OBV)

The on-balance volume, or OBV, is an indicator that estimates the volume trend for an asset. This indicator takes several volumes of information and adds them to become a single one-line indicator. The OBV measures cumulative selling or buying pressures by adding the volumes on up days and then subtract volume on down days.

Volume is an essential complementary measure used to verify price trends by determining whether they are happening on a high or a low number of trades. A falling price is usually accompanied by a falling OBV, while a rising price is accompanied by a rising OBV.

In cases where the OBV is rising while the price is not, there is a high possibility that the price will begin to rise like the OBV. If the OBV is falling or flat-lining while the price is rising, it is an indication that the price may be close to the top. In the same vein, If the OBV is rising or flat-lining while the price is falling, it is an indication that the price may be close to the bottom.

Chapter 11: Counter Trend Trading

Countertrend strategies are used to deduce a trend's possible reversal point. Traders who apply this approach are taking ideas from reversal candlestick patterns (pin bars, evening/morning starts, etc.) They also use oscillators like MACD or RSI to examine whether the market is overbought/oversold and whether there is a deviation between the indicator and the price.

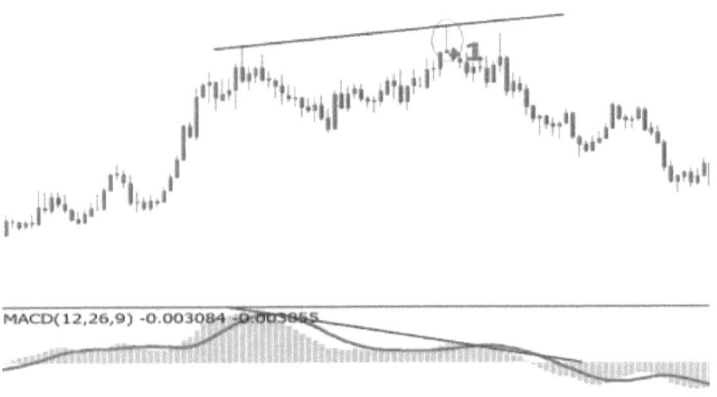

A trader may choose to sell at point 1 if the price formed a candle with a long upper shadow (a negative sign), and the MACD indicator didn't verify the price's high.

Countertrend trading is a medium-term strategy that traders use for several purposes like diversification, pure profit, and risk management.

Let's examine the following countertrend trading strategy terms:

Take profit: It's more difficult to find a place to fix profit when you trade countertrend. Note that you are betting against the market. Some trends can shift into a sideways market, restricting the profit of a countertrend position. The initial trend can as well resume fast and not let the price adjust excessively. Therefore, be cautious and manage the risks carefully.

Stop Loss: The position for a stop-loss order in such a trade is simple. Traders put their stop losses behind the ultimate point of the price from which an adjustment has started. The stop loss will possibly be shorter than the one you would apply if you trade the trend.

Scaling in: It's not an advisable idea to interfere with your position level when you trade the countertrend. The trade can be quite short-term, so you risk getting yourself in a difficult situation if you try to add to a trade. Be sure not to add to a losing position as it may result in a bigger loss.

Understanding Countertrend Trading

This is a trading method that attempts to make little gains by trading against the current market trade. Traders assume that the current trading trend will reverse, and they will make a profit from the reversal. This term, also called swing trading, refers to the opportunity to benefit from a trend that swings or reverses in a new direction.

This strategy is complex and usually used by only advanced traders for risk management and diversification.

Risk Management and Diversification

Active traders are mindful not to incur high risk on each of their trades; they usually limit the risk per trade to 2% and below of their portfolio.

On the other hand, advanced active traders who trade using technical signals, typically form grid trading strategies that place small trading bets all through a trend, which are specified at intervals for price decrease or increase to help them manage their risk. Theoretically, countertrend grid strategies that take inverse positions from the market can be one way for traders to manage their risks.

Some of these active contrarian traders prefer to focus on the countertrend trading method. They believe that buying into a bearish downtrend will benefit them when there is a bounce.

Chapter 12: Stock Scanning and Building an Effective Watchlist

Before we get started, we need to know the difference between a portfolio and a watchlist. The main distinction is that portfolios only list the stocks that belong to you while watchlists show securities and assets that you own alongside the ones that you've picked even if you've got no investment in them yet. Watchlist provides an insight into assets that you may wish to add to your portfolio at the end of the day.

To build an effective watchlist, a trader needs to understand how different sectors respond to catalysts over time, the impact of different levels of capitalization on price development, and an understanding of the modern market environment. There are several factors to consider when picking stocks that you want to follow daily, weekly, and monthly, factors like economic cycles, sentiment and seasonality.

Keep It Simple

Have different watchlist for the current factors and let these watchlists remind you of the research you put in place to arrive at them.

Review your list often – have a personal schedule of how often you want to review your list and check that the stock still suits your factors. Should they no longer suit your trading style, don't hesitate to delete the stock, to avoid being completely overwhelmed by an enormous list of stocks.

You can as well consider capping your list off at a number that's convenient for you to manage, so you don't have a high volume of stocks to watch.

Start Big, Then Go Small

You should start with wider sets of criteria for your research, and later, as you look at trends, you'll be able to cut down your criteria to suit your expectations. Besides, you must know what exactly you're looking for. This way, you can gradually weed out stocks that don't suit your trading patterns leaving you with a clean and effective database to work from.

The stock market consistently reinvents itself, so you always need to reinvent your list and adapt to changes swiftly. As with all stocks, your success is determined by the type of securities you're trading and the strategies you adopt.

Play Favorites

It's a brilliant idea to watch stocks that are already popular to find out why they became popular picks. Think of these as the bar that will in the future, set the stage for you to keep an eye on the downtrends and uptrends, so you can easily compare them to the stocks that you're planning to buy. Over time, you'll be able to leave these well-established companies and have your favorite stocks to watch.

Stay In The Know

Orchestrating an effective watchlist demands knowledge of the stock market. As soon as that understanding is reached, the results are worth the work that went into the research. Study to know how the changing levels of capitalization directly influence price actions and daily market development in general. Overtime, you'll nurture your investment pattern and get comfortable watching the trends of the stocks on your list. Stay put to a strategy, get up on the trends, and watch your stocks turn in profits.

Find What You Want

Scan the market and identify the specific factors you're seeking. There's a variety of factors to take into cognizance here, and your choices may change over time. Common rules of scanning include:

- Analyze patterns that indicate higher or lower trend changes.
- Analyze signals that measure any crucial unusual trends like, relatively low-price fluctuation with a high increase in average daily volume
- Analyze daily percentage fluctuation, especially if they have higher than average daily volume. Examples include stocks that have reached 52-week highs or 52-week lows.

Guidelines for Building a Watchlist

Watchlist requirements differ depending on the amount of time that an investor has available to trade and follow the financial market. A part-time trader does not need to go elaborate as he can have a list of 50 to 100 issues to track daily. However, full-time traders and market professionals need to spend more time studying the market, building a main database that has about 300 to

500 stocks, and another secondary list that can fit on the trading screen. Generally, each trading screen can display between 25 to 75 issues, depending on space used up by scanners, charts, market depth and news tickers.

Building a Database

You can have multiple sources that supply you stocks on your trading screens, but it is important to have an effective database that will provide the majority of these issues while making room for constant replenishment each time an asset is dropped due to shift in market tone, dull action or technical violations. After creating the database, the first thing to do is to add some of the market leaders from each major sector with the capitalization level down to two hundred and fifty million dollars. The next step will then be to create a list that contains your favorite stocks including popular stocks like those for amazon.com, Facebook, and Apple Inc.

Scanning the Market

Now, you are ready to scan the market in search of stocks that meet your trading pattern. After adding these issues to your database, you will now have an active list that you can rescan every night for precise setups and patterns while deleting stocks that you no longer want to follow.

Do not limit your criteria when you first begin to scan. The aim is to discover assets and stocks that you can follow daily or weekly. Use a combination of simple technical and fundamental criteria to identify and add stocks that may receive wide recognition in the nearest future.

Common Ways to Scan the Market

- Securities or assets that have low or high relative strength undergoing countertrend pullbacks.
- Candlesticks doji and hammers that detect one-bar reversals.
- Weak rallies into resistance in a downward trend.
- Popular breakdown and breakout signals.
- Percentage change in the last 30 days, five days or even today, filtered using the greater than average daily volume.

- Alarms that measure unusual activities. An example is a three to five times average daily volume with little or no change in price.

Chapter 13: 3-Step Day Trading Plan

In the quest for knowledge and making money real big, a lot of new day traders forget the most crucial steps in gaining profitability and consistency, and that is 'practice.'

To achieve consistent profitability with day trading, you must dedicate a lot of time to monitor market movements effectively. And that's how your trading skills will improve. You can simply think of it as your new job. If becoming a day trader is your dream, you'll need to abide by these three essential day trading tips.

Prepare thoroughly

Day trading attracts a lot of controversies with some traders who argue that it is more like gambling rather than investing, and it can be particularly challenging for newbies. Successful day traders are basically professionals who have shaped their careers around constant practicing and intensive research.

Preparation is key for any new pursuit, and you'll have to go the extra mile when it comes to day trading. Before anything, you'll need to set a strict budget that you want to risk on the market. Good thing, you don't need as much capital to start day trading as you would for several other types of trades.

A minimum of $25,000 is required to be in your account to begin day trading. You should ensure that you never risk more than one or two percent of your account on any single trade. You also need to concentrate on just one or two patterns or strategies in the beginning until you have a deep understanding of the market.

Lastly, you must understand that your gains will in no doubt, be smaller than other forms of trading, and they will still be taxed. Like every other form of trading, you'll also take losses on trades, maybe even frequently. This is very much possible, especially when you make moves during the more volatile trade hours, but it's important to stay put to your strategy once you start trading for the day. No trading plan is perfect for all time and you must be ready to adapt to quick changes in market trends.

Know when to sell

It's always good to be on the winning side, and there are several different ways to spot one. The ability to spot the most profitable one is essential to maximize profits.

Scalping is one of the most advisable day trading approaches as it yields more profit than you would on a position. This is probably the safest choice, but the downside is that it has a lower profit margin.

Daily pivots are surely profitable but will involve studying an option for some time. The idea is to understand when the price will drop to its lowest during its volatile time of the day, and then sell it when the price has reached its highest.

Momentum trading is not common among day traders. But it is possible to buy stocks according to news releases of the day and then sell them for a profit before the day's trading is over.

Limit losses

You must always find a way to dodge huge losses from unpromising trades. A stop-loss order will be the best option for this: this is an order you can set to shut down your positions automatically whenever prices drop too low. Supposedly, you buy stocks for $12 per share, you can set a stop-loss order to close out your position in case the price drop below $11; thus, still maintaining a bearable risk. You can place well-set orders to automatically sell positions as soon as their value is high enough. This can be beneficial for periods when you can't watch price actions yourself.

www.ingramcontent.com/pod-product-compliance
Lightning Source LLC
Chambersburg PA
CBHW030707220526
45463CB00005B/1937